TOEFL Reading Practice Book
Reading Preparation
for the TOEFL iBT
and Paper Delivered Tests

TOEFL® and TOEFL iBT® are registered trademarks of Educational Testing Service (ETS). This publication is not associated with or endorsed by ETS.

TOEFL Reading Practice Book: Reading Preparation for the TOEFL iBT and Paper Delivered Tests

© COPYRIGHT 2018. Exam SAM Study Aids and Media. www.examsam.com

All rights reserved. No part of this publication may be reproduced, stored in a retrieval system, or transmitted, in any form or by any means, electronic, mechanical, photocopying, recording or otherwise.

TOEFL® and TOEFL iBT® are registered trademarks of Educational Testing Service (ETS). This publication is not associated with or endorsed by ETS.

TABLE OF CONTENTS

TOEFL Reading Exam Question Types

Basic Comprehension	1
Language Use	1
Reading to Learn	2

TOEFL iBT Reading Comprehension – Practice Test 1

Test 1 – Part 1	4
Test 1 – Part 2	13
Test 1 – Part 3	23
Test 1 – Answer Key	32
Test 1 – Answers and Explanations	33

TOEFL iBT Reading Comprehension – Practice Test 2

Test 2 – Part 1	41
Test 2 – Part 2	51
Test 2 – Part 3	61
Test 2 – Answer Key	70
Test 2 – Answers and Explanations	71

TOEFL iBT Reading Comprehension – Practice Test 3

Test 3 – Part 1	78
Test 3 – Part 2	87
Test 3 – Part 3	97

Test 3 – Answer Key 106

Test 3 – Answers and Explanations 107

TOEFL Reading Exam Question Types

Reading questions on the TOEFL iBT and Paper-Delivered Reading Exams can be placed into the following categories:

BASIC COMPREHENSION:

1) Main idea questions – You will need to understand the main idea of the passage or of a certain paragraph for these types of questions. You may need to choose your answer from multiple choice options or you may need to match headings or titles with certain sections of the passage.

2) Reading for detail questions – For these types of questions, you will need to scan the passage for the information required and then answer the question. Reading for detail questions can be of any of the following formats: multiple choice, short answer, sentence completion, matching, or form or diagram completion.

3) Making inferences – These questions are not as common as main idea or specific detail questions; however, students often consider inference questions to be the most difficult ones. Inference questions will ask you to find out what idea is implied or indirectly expressed in the passage.

LANGUAGE USE:

3) Coherence – In this type of question, you will see a new sentence. You then need to choose the best place to put the new sentence in the passage.

5) Rhetorical function – This type of question will ask you why the author includes a certain detail or example in the passage. Typical answers to this type of question include: giving an example, explaining a detail, or supporting a claim.

6) Word meaning – You will also see questions on inferring word meaning. For these types of questions, you will see a word in bold in the reading comprehension passage. You will then be asked to choose the best synonym for the word, based upon the context of the passage.

7) Locating a referent – For this type of question, a phrase will be highlighted in the passage. You need to understand what the phrase is referring to, and then choose the best explanation from the choices provided.

8) Defining a key term – You will see a specialized or technical term highlighted in the passage. You will need to choose the best definition for the term from the choices provided

9) Paraphrasing – This type of question will include an excerpt from the reading passage and ask you to select the best paraphrase of it from the answer choices provided.

READING TO LEARN:

10) Author's attitude or opinion – You may be asked about the author's opinion or attitude on the subject of the passage.

11) Summarizing – You will need to select the group of statements that best express the most important main ideas from the passage.

12) Understanding details – You will be asked how a specific point relates to the main idea of the passage.

Each of the practice tests in his publication contains all of the above types of questions on the real TOEFL iBT and paper-delivered tests.

TOEFL iBT Reading Comprehension – Practice Test 1

Instructions: The reading test contains 3 parts (39 total questions). You have 60 minutes to complete all three parts of the reading test.

Reading Test Part 1:

Tornadoes

[1] Although improved weather observation practices seem to have reduced the severity of tornadoes in recent years, they continue to be one of the most severe types of weather-related events. While many people live in fear of tornadoes and the path of destruction they wreak, very few people actually understand how these weather events occur. Even fewer people understand how to protect themselves and their property if a tornado were to strike.

[2] Tornadoes develop as the wind changes direction and the wind speed simultaneously increases. This combination of atmospheric changes results in spinning movements in the troposphere, which is the lowest level of the earth's atmosphere. The resulting **whirling** motion, which sometimes is not even visible to the observer, is compounded when the rotating air column moves to a vertical position. The developing tornado draws in warm air surrounding it at ground level, and its speed begins to increase. As warm air is drawn in, a funnel is

produced that extends from the cloud above it to the earth below. The resulting funnels thus become **pendent** from low-pressure areas of storm clouds.

[3] When a tornado touches the ground, a strong upward draft, which is called a vortex, is formed. The vortex is a circular, rolling column of wind that reaches speeds of more than 200 miles per hour. As it moves across the landscape, the tornado creates a path of destruction. **These twisters** have been known to lift heavy objects, such as large animals or cars, and cast them off several miles away. Houses that are hit by tornadoes appear to explode as the normal air pressure inside the building collides with the low air pressure inside the vortex.

[4] Tornadoes can appear any time of the year, but they are most common during the summer. Further, while they usually occur between 3:00 PM and 9:00 PM, tornadoes can, in theory, happen at any time of the day. Even though these twisting funnels have been witnessed in many places in the world, they are the most common in the United States. {A *} On average, there are 1,200 tornadoes annually in this nation, causing 70 deaths and 1,500 injuries.

[5] In spite of having **myriad** sizes and shapes, tornadoes are normally classified as weak, strong, or violent. It is notable that the majority of all tornadoes are

categorized as weak. To be classified as a weak tornado, the duration of the event must be less than 10 minutes and the speed must be under 110 miles per hour. Strong tornadoes, which comprise approximately 10 percent of all twisters, may have durations of more than 20 minutes each and speeds of up to 205 miles per hour. Violent tornadoes are the rarest since they occur less than one percent of the time. Although uncommon, violent tornadoes last for more than one hour and result in the greatest loss of life. {B *} While a violent tornado can destroy a solidly-constructed, well-built home, weak tornadoes can also cause a great deal of damage.

[6] Because of the destructive, powerful nature of tornadoes, there are many myths and misconceptions about them. For example, some people hold the view that tornadoes cannot occur over oceans, lakes, or rivers. However, **waterspouts**, tornadoes that develop over bodies of water, can in many cases cause major damage to coastal areas as they move onshore. Additionally, tornadoes can take place concurrently with tropical storms and hurricanes as they move to land. Another myth is that damage to structures such as office complexes and houses can be prevented if their windows are opened before the storm strikes. Founded on the mistaken belief that open windows can equalize the pressure inside the

building and prevent damage to it, this action can instead cause severe injury or death. {C *}

[7] Because tornadoes have serious consequences for communities and their inhabitants, safety measures are of the utmost importance during severe weather conditions. Drivers sometimes try to outrun tornadoes in their vehicles, but it is very dangerous to do so. Cars and other vehicles offer very little protection when tornadoes hit, so drivers should leave their vehicles and look for safe shelter. Mobile homes and trailers also afford little shelter, so residents of these types of dwellings should go to an underground floor of the nearest building. {D *} In the event that a building has no subterranean level, a person should then find the lowest floor of a nearby building and position him- or herself under a heavy object. If no building is located nearby, a person stuck in a tornado can lie prostrate in a nearby ditch or other low area of land and protect his or her head.

1. The best synonym for the word **whirling** in the passage is:

   A. visible

   B. rotating

   C. dancing

   D. worsening

2. The best synonym for the word **pendent** in the passage is:

    A. churning

    B. increasing

    C. hanging

    D. level

3. Which of the following sentences provides the best paraphrase of this sentence from paragraph 3?

    As it moves across the landscape, the tornado creates a path of destruction.

    A. The tornado causes enormous damage to beautifully landscaped parks and gardens.

    B. The tornado's damage most commonly occurs in municipalities that have been landscaped.

    C. The tornado causes damage to wide-open areas; however, the damage is not normally very severe.

    D. As the tornado travels across the countryside, it creates a long trail of damage.

4. In paragraph 3, the words **these twisters** refer to:

    A. tornadoes

B. a path of destruction

C. the landscape

D. the extent of damage

5. All of the following key facts about tornadoes are mentioned in paragraph 4 except:

    A. the yearly number of deaths in the US from tornadoes

    B. the time of day when tornadoes usually take place

    C. the time of year when tornadoes are most common

    D. the average wind speed of most tornadoes

6. The word **myriad** in the passage is closest in meaning to:

    A. limited

    B. extreme

    C. many

    D. average

7. In paragraph 5, what is the author's main purpose?

    A. to explain how tornadoes are classified

    B. to identify the most frequent type of tornadoes

C. to emphasize the loss of life and damage to property caused by tornadoes

D. to compare weak tornadoes to strong tornadoes

8. Based on the information contained in paragraph 6, which of the following best explains the term **waterspouts**?

A. Tornadoes that move away from coastal areas

B. Tornadoes that occur over oceans, rivers, and lakes

C. Tornadoes that occur onshore

D. Tornadoes that accompany tropical storms and hurricanes

9. Look at the four stars { * } that indicate where the following sentence could be added to the passage.

Indeed, the highest number of deaths and injuries are not caused by the winds themselves, but by flying debris, such as broken glass from open windows.

Where is the best place to insert this new sentence?

A. {A *}

B. {B *}

C. {C *}

D. {D *}

10. According to paragraph 6, what can be inferred about the public's knowledge about tornadoes?

    A.   A large number of people know how to avoid tornado damage.

    B.   Most people appreciate the risk of death associated with tornadoes.

    C.   Some members of the public know how to regulate the pressure inside buildings.

    D.   A number of people are not fully aware of certain key information about tornadoes, especially about tornado safety.

11. What is the safest place to be when a tornado strikes?

    A.   an abandoned vehicle

    B.   mobile homes

    C.   the basement of a building

    D.   under a piece of sturdy furniture

12. According to the passage, tornadoes are considered to be a severe weather phenomenon because:

    A.   many people fear them.

    B.   they produce strong vortexes.

    C.   they can be placed into three discrete categories.

    D.   they can result in death and devastation.

13. Select the answer below that represents the two most important ideas contained in the passage.

    A. (i) Tornadoes can cause catastrophic loss in terms of life and property.

        (ii) Everyone should be educated about what to do in the event of a tornado.

    B. (i) Most tornadoes occur in the afternoon.

        (ii) Few tornadoes are violent.

    C. (i) Some members of the public are ill-informed about when and where tornadoes can occur.

        (ii) Sheltering in a ditch is a last resort if a tornado should strike.

    D. (i) Most tornadoes occur in the afternoon.

        (ii) Everyone should be educated about what to do in the event of a tornado.

Reading Test Part 2:

Child Development

[1] Jean Piaget is one of the most well-known theorists in child development and educational psychology, and the scholastic community still discusses his principles today. Focusing his research on the processes by which human beings learn how to exist in their environments, Piaget strived to answer the question: "How do human beings obtain knowledge?" He is responsible for discovering what he termed "**abstract symbolic reasoning**." This term refers to the notion that biology impacts upon child development much more than socialization. Piaget determined that younger children responded to research questions differently than older children. His conclusion was that different responses occurred not because younger children were less intelligent, but because they were at a lower level of biological development. **{A *}**

[2] As a biologist, Piaget had an intense curiosity in the manner in which organisms adapted to their environments, and this interest resulted in several revolutionary theories. Piaget postulated that children's behaviors were regulated by mental structures called "schemes," which enable a child to interpret the world and respond appropriately to new situations. Piaget observed the process by which human beings have to learn how use their mental structures as they become familiarized with their environments, and he **coined** the term "equilibration" to describe this process.

[3] The biologist noted that all children are born with the drive to adapt, and he therefore posited that mental schemes of adaptation are innate. While an animal continues to use its in-born adaptation schemes throughout its entire existence, human beings, in Piaget's view, have innate schemes that compete with and then bifurcate from constructed schemes, which are those that are acquired as one interacts with and adapts to his or her social environment. {B *}

[4] The process of adaptation, which is split into the two distinct functions of assimilation and accommodation, was of paramount importance in Piaget's research. The function of assimilation refers to the way in which a person transforms the environment in order to utilize innate cognitive schemes and structures. Alternatively, the **latter function** is used to describe the way in which pre-existing schemes or mental structures are altered in the process of accepting the conditions of one's environment. For example, the schemes used in bottle feeding or breast feeding a baby illustrate the process of of assimilation because the child utilizes his or her innate ability to for suckle to carry out both tasks.

Further, when a child begins to eat with a spoon rather than a bottle, he or she uses accommodation since a completely new way of eating must be learned.

[5] As Piaget's body of research expanded, he identified four developmental stages of cognition in children. In the first stage, which he called the sensorimotor stage, Piaget observed that at the **incipience** of the child's cognitive development, intelligence is demonstrated in the manner in which the infant interacts physically with the world. In other words, intelligence is directly related to mobility and motor activity at this stage. In addition, children start to obtain language skills and memory, which Piaget termed "object permanence," in this initial developmental stage. {C *}

[6] As a toddler, the child begins the pre-operational stage, which is quite **egocentric**, so most of his or her intellectual and emotional energy is self-centered rather than empathetic at this point of development. {D *} Although intelligence, language, and memory continue developing during this time, thinking is mainly inflexible and illogical.

[7] The concrete operational stage begins at approximately age 5. Logical and systematic thought processes appear during this stage, and the child begins to

comprehend measurement and symbols pertaining to concrete objects, such as numbers, amounts, volumes, lengths, and weights. The egocentrism of the previous stage begins to diminish during the concrete operational stage as thinking becomes more logical.

[8] The final stage, termed the formal operational stage, begins at the start of the teenage years. This stage is normally characterized by abstract thought on a wide range of complex ideas and theories. However, research has indicated that adults in many countries have not completed this stage due to the lack of educational opportunities or poverty.

14. Based upon paragraph 1, which is the best explanation for the term **abstract symbolic reasoning**?

    A.   Older children are more intelligent than younger children.

    B.   Older children are more physically developed that younger children.

    C.   Older children are more socially developed than younger children.

    D.   The intellectual development of children is affected by their biological development.

15. The best synonym for the term **coined** is:

    A.   realized

    B.   recovered

    C.   invented

    D.   utilized

16. According to paragraph 2, the following statements about Piaget are true except:

    A.   Piaget's work as a biologist had a profound impact upon his research on child development.

    B.   Piaget understood that mental development is closely connected to biological development.

    C.   Piaget realized that biological factors affected child development, in addition to environmental factors.

    D.   Piaget was the very first researcher on the subject of child development.

17. The best synonym for the word **incipience** in the passage is:

    A.   start

    B.   prime

C. mental

D. active

18. The best synonym for the word **egocentric** in the passage is:

    A. shy

    B. selfish

    C. uninformed

    D. illogical

19. Look at the four stars { * } that indicate where the following sentence could be added to the passage.

    Further, as schemes become more complex due to this cycle of interaction and adaptation, they are termed "structures."

    Where is the best place to insert this new sentence?

    A. {A *}

    B. {B *}

    C. {C *}

    D. {D *}

20. Which of the sentences below is the best paraphrase of the following sentence from paragraph 3?

While an animal continues to use its in-born adaptation schemes throughout its entire existence, human beings, in Piaget's view, have innate schemes that compete with and then bifurcate from constructed schemes, which are those that are acquired as one interacts with and adapts to his or her social environment.

   A. Piaget theorized that, unlike the schemes of other animals, human being's schemes are primarily acquired in the socialization process.

   B. In contrast to other animals, human beings use their innate schemes throughout their lifetimes, rather than departing from constructed schemes.

   C. The process by which human beings acquire schemes is different than that of other animals because human beings acquire schemes during the socialization process, and these acquired schemes diverge from their innate schemes.

   D. Piaget noted that human beings differ to other animals since they do not rely only on in-born cognitive mechanisms.

21. The words the **latter function** in the passage refer to:

    A. assimilation

    B. transformation

    C. conformance

    D. accommodation

22. Why does the author mention bottle feeding in paragraph 4 of the passage?

    A. To identify one of the important features of assimilation

    B. To exemplify the assimilation process

    C. To describe the importance of assimilation

    D. To explain difficulties children face during assimilation

23. According to the passage, which of the following statements best characterizes the sensorimotor stage?

    A. The growth of the child's intelligence in this stage depends predominantly on his or her verbal ability.

    B. The skills obtained during this stage are of less importance than those achieved during later developmental stages.

C. During this stage, the child learns how his or her mobility relates to language.

D. The child's cognitive development in this stage is achieved through physical movement in his or her environment.

24. Based on the information in paragraphs 6 and 7, what can be inferred about child development?

   A. Before the child enters the concrete operational stage, his or her thinking is largely rigid and unsystematic.

   B. The conceptualization of symbols is not as important as the conceptualization of numbers.

   C. The child becomes more egocentric during the concrete operational stage.

   D. Memory and language become less important during the concrete operational stage.

25. According to the passage, the formal operational stage:

   A. is the result of poor economic conditions.

   B. has not yet been finished by many individuals around the world.

   C. is an important global problem.

   D. in no way is connected to the availability of education.

26. What is the author's main purpose?

   A. To provide biographical information about Jean Piaget

   B. To discuss the significant aspects of Jean Piaget's theories on child development

   C. To criticize the research of Jean Piaget

   D. To point out flaws in current child development theory

Reading Test Part 3:

Archeology

[1] The discipline of archeology has been developing since wealthy European men began to **plunder** relics from distant lands in the early nineteenth century. Initially considered an upper-class hobby, archeology in general and archeological field methods in particular have undergone many developments and experienced many challenges in recent years.

[2] Before the field excavation begins, a **viable** site must first be located. While this process can involve assiduous research, sometimes sheer luck or an archeologist's instinctive hunch also come into play. A logical locality to begin searching is one near sites in which artifacts have been found previously. Failing that, an archeologist must consider, at a minimum, whether the potential site would have been habitable for people in antiquity. {A *} Bearing in mind that modern conveniences and facilities like electricity and running water were not available in pre-historic times, the archeologist quickly discerns that sites near rivers and caves could provide the water and shelter indispensable for day-to-day living in such inhospitable conditions.

[3] Once the site has been located, the process of surveying commences. This means that the ground surface of the site is visually scrutinized to determine whether any artifacts are protruding through the soil. The archeologist then digs test pits, small holes that are equidistant to one another, to determine what the boundaries of the larger final pit will be. Once these dimensions are determined, the hole is dug and sectioned off with rope or plastic.

[4] The excavation, which is a meticulous and lengthy process, then begins in full. The archeologist must gauge the texture and color of the soil carefully as the pit becomes deeper and deeper since variations in soil composition can be used to identify climatic and other living conditions. It is imperative that the walls of the excavation are kept uniformly straight as the dig progresses so that **these differences** can be identified.

[5] The soil that is removed from the pit is sifted through a sieve or similar device, consisting of a screen that is suspended across a metal or wooden frame. After the soil is placed in the sieve, the archeologist gently **oscillates** the device. As the mechanism goes back and forth in this way, the soil falls to the ground below, while larger objects are caught in the screen. {B *}

[6] Throughout this process, all findings are entered in a written record to ensure that every artifact is cataloged. This activity can certainly be tedious; yet, it is one that is critical in order to account for each and every item properly. Each finding is placed in a plastic bag bearing a catalog number. Subsequent to this, a map of the excavation site is produced, on which the exact in-situ location of every artifact is indicated by level and position.

[7] Finally, the arduous task of interpreting the findings ensues. During the last two centuries, various approaches have been utilized in this respect. Throughout the early 1800's, most fossil recovery took place on the European continent, resulting in an extremely Euro-centric method of examination and dissemination of findings. {C *} Unfortunately, as a consequence, the misapprehension that the origins of homo-sapiens were European began to take shape both in the archeological and wider communities.

[8] Recent research suggests that inherent social and cultural biases pervaded the manner in which archeological findings were investigated and explicated during the early nineteenth century because little attention was paid to the roles that wealth, status, and nationality played in the interpretation of the artifacts.

{D *} These problems began to be surmounted, however, in the 1860's, with the advent of the theories of Charles Darwin on the origin of the human species.

[9] Darwinian theory, the notion that human beings are the ultimate product of a long biological evolutionary process, then infiltrated the discipline of archeology and heavily influenced the manner in which archeological artifacts were recovered and analyzed. By the middle of the 1900's, the imbalance created by the cultural biases began to be rectified as there was a surge in artifacts excavated from African and Asian localities.

27. The word **plunder** in this passage is closest in meaning to:

    A. take

    B. leave

    C. accept

    D. notice

28. The word **viable** in this passage is closest in meaning to:

    A. collectable

    B. prominent

    C. workable

    D. careful

29. The words **these differences** in this passage refer to:

    A. climatic conditions

    B. soil variations

    C. excavation walls

    D. dig progression

30. According to the passage, what do archeologists consider when choosing a potential site for excavation?

    A. whether research can be conducted on the site

    B. whether electricity is presently available

    C. whether the site existed in pre-historic times

    D. whether any data was previously collected from areas near the site

31. Look at the four stars { * } that indicate where the following sentence could be added to the passage.

    Bones, stones, fossils, and tools are artifacts that are typically found during the excavation process.

    Where is the best place to insert this new sentence?

    A. {A *}

    B. {B *}

    C. {C *}

    D. {D *}

32. The word **oscillates** in this passage is closest in meaning to:

    A. inculcates

    B. exculpates

    C. manipulates

    D. vibrates

33. Why are artifacts recorded in a written catalog?

    A. to ensure that no items are lost

    B. to prepare a map of the site

    C. to understand the item's in-situ location

    D. to prepare them for long-term storage in plastic containers

34. Which of the following statements accurately expresses the author's attitude about the Euro-centric method mentioned in paragraph 7?

    A. It was regrettable, but necessary.

    B. It was completely unavoidable.

    C. It was regrettable because it created cultural misunderstandings.

    D. It only took place within a small geographical area.

35. In paragraph 8, the author discusses biases in order to:

    A. criticize wealthy nineteenth century archeologists.

    B. clarify to effect of archeology on culture.

    C. explain how these problems affected the analysis and interpretation of artifacts.

    D. shed light on the ideas of Charles Darwin.

36. Based on the information contained in paragraph 9, what can be inferred about the early 1900s?

    A. There were few archeological findings from Africa and Asia.

    B. Darwinian theory had little effect on archeology.

    C. All archeological findings were culturally imbalanced.

    D. Charles Darwin recovered many artifacts.

37. According to the passage, archeological methods

    A. have developed a good deal when compared to earlier centuries.

    B. need to remain static to be useful.

    C. should help to create cultural differences.

    D. have been rectified in countries in the Far East.

38. Summarize the passage by selecting the group of sentences below that express the three most important ideas contained in the passage:

    A.   (i) An archeologist has many things to consider when selecting a site.

          (ii) Protruding artifacts can create difficulties during the excavation.

          (iii) The European archeological discoveries of the 1800's should be disregarded.

    B.   (i) Protruding artifacts can create difficulties during the excavation.

          (ii) Preparing written archeological records is tedious.

          (iii) Cultural prejudices should be avoided when archeological findings are being interpreted.

    C.   (i) An archeologist has many things to consider when selecting a site.

          (ii) The excavation of an archeological site is a meticulous and methodical process.

          (iii) Cultural prejudices should be avoided when archeological findings are being interpreted.

    D.   (i) The excavation of an archeological site is a meticulous and methodical process.

          (ii) Preparing written archeological records is tedious.

(iii) The European archeological discoveries of the 1800's should be disregarded.

39. The passage you have read discusses archeological field methods, as well as archeological developments. Look at the answers below, and choose the one to which archeological field methods are related.

    A.   (i) site selection

           (ii) site excavation

    B.   (i) site excavation

           (ii) artifact interpretation

    C.   (i) artifact interpretation

           (ii) Darwinian theory

    D.   (i) Darwinian theory

           (ii) site selection

TOEFL Practice Reading – Test 1
Answer Key

1. B
2. C
3. D
4. A
5. D
6. C
7. A
8. B
9. C
10. D
11. C
12. D
13. A
14. D
15. C
16. D
17. A
18. B
19. B
20. C

21. D
22. B
23. D
24. A
25. B
26. B
27. A
28. C
29. B
30. D
31. B
32. D
33. A
34. C
35. C
36. A
37. A
38. C
39. A

TOEFL Practice Reading – Test 1 Answers and Explanations

1) The correct answer is B. "Whirling" has the same meaning as "spinning," which is used in the previous sentence in this paragraph.

2) The correct answer is C. The sentence before this one states that "a funnel is produced that extends from the cloud above it to the earth below." So, we know that the funnel hangs from the cloud.

3) The correct answer is D. The phrase "creates a path of destruction" refers to an event that causes extensive damage. The word "landscape" in this sentence refers to the countryside in a particular geographic region. The word "landscaped" in the answer choices is used to describe lawns and gardens.

4) The correct answer is A. We have read that tornadoes have a twisting or whirling movement. We also know answer A is correct because the two previous sentences in this paragraph talk about tornadoes.

5) The correct answer is D. Paragraph 4 states that tornadoes cause 70 deaths each year in the US. It also states that tornadoes "usually occur between 3:00 PM and 9:00 PM." Finally, the paragraph mentions that tornadoes are most common during the summer. Wind speed is not mentioned until paragraph 5.

6) The correct answer is C. Because of the phrase "normally classified" in the same sentence, we know that we are making a general rule based on many individual events of tornadoes.

7) The correct answer is A. The author's purpose is stated in the first two sentences of this paragraph: "Tornadoes are normally classified as weak, strong, or violent. It is notable that the majority of all tornadoes are categorized as weak."

8) The correct answer is B. The phrase after the word "waterspouts" provides the meaning of this word: "tornadoes that develop over bodies of water."

9) The correct answer is C. The previous sentence in paragraph 6 refers to open windows, so the new sentence continues the line of reasoning about the danger of open windows.

10) The correct answer is D. Paragraph 6 talks about myths and misconceptions. Both of these words mean that people do not possess factual information about a certain topic.

11) The correct answer is C. Paragraph 7 states: "Cars and other vehicles offer very little protection when tornadoes hit, so drivers should leave their vehicles and look for safe shelter. Mobile homes and trailers also afford little shelter, so

residents of these types of dwellings should go to an underground floor of the nearest building." The basement is the underground floor of a building.

12) The correct answer is D. The passage mainly discusses the loss of life and property caused by tornadoes. Answer choices A, B, and C are specific points from the passage.

13) The correct answer is A. The passage mentions the two ideas summarized in answer choice A. The other information in answer choices B, C, and D is mentioned in the passage as specific points, not main ideas.

14) The correct answer is D. Paragraph 1 states: "Piaget determined that younger children responded to research questions differently than older children. His conclusion was that different responses occurred not because younger children were less intelligent, but because they were at a lower level of biological development." In other words, he linked their intellectual ability to their biological development.

15) The correct answer is C. "Coin a term" means to invent a new word or term.

16) The correct answer is D. Answer A is true because the first sentence of paragraph 2 talks about Piaget's work as a biologist. Answer B is true since the second sentence of paragraph 2 describes Piaget's discovery of mental schemes. Answer C is true because the last sentence of paragraph 2 provides

details about environmental adaptation. The paragraph does not state that Piaget was the first researcher in this field, so choice D is not true.

17) The correct answer is A. The second sentence of this paragraph states that the sensorimotor stage is the first stage.

18) The correct answer is B. The next part of the sentence states that: "his or her intellectual and emotional energy is self-centered rather than empathetic." Self-centered is a synonym for selfish.

19) The correct answer is B. The schemes are mentioned for the first time in paragraph 3, so the new sentence needs to be placed in this paragraph.

20) The correct answer is C. The sentence mentions both the social environment and the idea of bifurcation, or division. Sentence C mentions both of these ideas, but the other answer choices do not mention both of them.

21) The correct answer is D. "Latter" means the last thing mentioned. Accommodation is the last function mentioned in the first sentence of paragraph 4.

22) The correct answer is B. "Exemplify" means to give an example. Bottle feeding is given as an example in paragraph 4 because this idea is introduced by using the phrase "for example."

23) The correct answer is D. Paragraph 5 mentions that in this stage "intelligence is demonstrated in the manner in which the infant interacts physically with the world." The words "mobility" and "motor activity" in this paragraph also express the idea of physical movement. Note that "cognitive" means intellectual.

24) The correct answer is A. Paragraph 7 mention that "logical and systematic thought processes appear" during the concrete operational stage. Since these skills appear during the concrete operational stage, they don't exist prior to this time.

25) The correct answer is B. Paragraph 8 states: "adults in many countries have not completed this stage due to the lack of educational opportunities or poverty."

26) The correct answer is B. The author's purpose is clearly stated in the first sentence of the passage: "Jean Piaget is one of the most well-known theorists in child development and educational psychology, and the scholastic community still discusses his principles today."

27) The correct answer is A. The meaning of this word can be inferred from the other paragraphs in the passage. We know from the other paragraphs in the passage that archeologists take items from the places that they dig up.

28) The correct answer is C. The meaning of this word can also be inferred from other paragraphs in the passage. Paragraphs 4, 5, and 6 talk about the way in which archeologists work once they have found a site.

29) The correct answer is B. "These differences" refers to the phrase "variations in soil composition" which is mentioned in the previous sentence in paragraph 4.

30) The correct answer is D. Paragraph 2 states: "A logical locality to begin searching is one near sites in which artifacts have been found previously."

31) The correct answer is B. Paragraph 5 discusses how objects are recovered from the site. Because the sentence from above describes the kinds of objects that are usually discovered, it should be placed at the end of paragraph 5.

32) The correct answer is D. The meaning of this word is revealed in the next sentence in paragraph 5: "the mechanism goes back and forth in this way . . ."

33) The correct answer is A. Sentence 2 of paragraph 6 states that cataloging "can certainly be tedious; yet, it is one that is critical in order to account for each and every item properly." The phrase "account for" means to be sure that every item is present, or stated conversely, to be sure that no item is missing.

34) The correct answer is C. The last sentence of paragraph 7 states: "Unfortunately, as a consequence, the misapprehension that the origins of homo sapiens were European began to take shape both in the archeological and wider

communities." The word "unfortunately" makes it clear that this action is regrettable. The words "misunderstanding" and "misapprehension" are synonyms. The phrase "wider communities" means culturally.

35) The correct answer is C. The first sentence of paragraph 8 states: "social and cultural biases pervaded the manner in which archeological findings were investigated and explicated during the early nineteenth century . . ." "Pervade" means to affect extensively. "Explicate" means explain.

36) The correct answer is A. The last paragraph states: "By the middle of the 1900's, [. . .] there was a surge in artifacts excavated from African and Asian localities." Since there was a surge or sudden increase in the discovery of artifacts from Asia and Africa around the 1950's, we can conclude that there were few archeological findings from these areas previously.

37) The correct answer is A. This is a main idea question. The main idea of this passage is stated in the first sentence: "The discipline of archeology has been developing since wealthy European men began to plunder relics from distant lands in the early nineteenth century."

38) The correct answer is C. The passage discusses the three main ideas stated in choice C. The following statement in choices A and D is false according to the passage: "The European archeological discoveries of the 1800s should be

disregarded." The other ideas mentioned in choices A, B, and D are true according to the passage, but they are specific points, not main ideas.

39) The correct answer is A. Artifact interpretation and Darwinian theory are archeological developments, not archeological field methods.

TOEFL iBT Reading Comprehension – Practice Test 2

Instructions: The reading test contains 3 parts (40 total questions). You have 60 minutes to complete all three parts of the reading test.

Reading Test Part 1:

Gravity

[1] The question of the mechanics of motion is complex and one that has a protracted history. Indeed, much has been discovered about gravity, defined as the force that draws objects to the earth, both before and since the British mathematician Sir Isaac Newton mused upon the subject in the 17th century. As early as the third century BC, a Greek philosopher and natural scientist named Aristotle conducted a great deal of scientific investigation into the subject. Most of Aristotle's life was devoted to the study of the objects of natural science, and it is for this work that he is most **renowned**. The Greek scientist wrote a tome entitled *Metaphysics*, which contains the observations that he made as a result of performing this original research in the natural sciences.

[2] Several centuries later, in the first century AD, Ptolemy, another Greek scientist, was credited with a **nascent**, yet unformulated theory, that there was a force that moved toward the center of the earth, thereby holding objects on its

surface. Although later ridiculed for his belief that the earth was the center of the planetary system, **Aristotle's compatriot** nevertheless did contribute to the development of the theory of gravity. {A *}

[3] However, it was during the period called the Renaissance that gravitational forces were perhaps studied most widely. An astronomer, Galileo Galilei corrected one of Aristotle's erring theories by pointing out that objects of differing weights fall to earth at the same speed. Years later, Descartes, who was known at that time as a dilettante philosopher, but was later dubbed the father of modern mathematics, held that a body in circular motion constantly strives to recede from the center. This theory gave credence to the notion that bodies in motion had their own forces.

[4] Newton took these studies a step further, and used them to show that the earth's rotation does not fling bodies into the air because the force of gravity, measured by the rate of falling bodies, is greater than the centrifugal force arising from the rotation. In his first mathematical formulation of gravity, published in 1687, Newton posited that the same force that kept the moon from being propelled away from the earth also applied to gravity at the earth's surface. {B *}

While this finding, termed the Law of Universal Gravitation, is said to have been occasioned by Newton's observation of the fall of an apple from a tree in the orchard at his home, in reality, the idea did not come to the scientist in a flash of inspiration, but was developed slowly over time.

[5] Newton had the **prescience** to appreciate that his study was of great importance for the scientific community and for society as a whole. It is because of Newton's work that we currently understand the effect of gravity on the earth as a global system. For instance, as a result of Newton's investigation into the subject of gravity, we know today that geological features such as mountains and canyons can cause variances in the Earth's gravitational force. {C *} Newton must also be acknowledged for the realization that the force of gravity becomes less robust as the distance from the equator diminishes, due to the rotation of the earth, as well as the declining mass and density of the planet from the equator to the poles.

[6] In spite of these discoveries, Newton remained perplexed throughout his lifetime by the causes of the power implied by the variables of his mathematical equations on gravity. In other words, he was unable adequately to explain the natural forces upon which the power of gravity relied. Even though he tried to

justify these forces by describing them merely as phenomena of nature, differing hypotheses on these phenomena still abound today. {D *}

[7] In 1915, Albert Einstein addressed Newton's reservations by developing the revolutionary theory of general relativity. Einstein asserted that the paths of objects in motion can sometimes deviate, or change direction over the course of time, as a result of the curvature of space time. Numerous subsequent investigations into and tests of the theory of general relativity have unequivocally supported Einstein's groundbreaking work.

1. The word **renowned** in the passage is closest in meaning to

    A. despised

    B. known

    C. welcomed

    D. important

2. The word **nascent** in the passage is closest in meaning to

    A. newly formed

    B. old fashioned

    C. widely accepted

    D. obviously untrue

3. The phrase **Aristotle's compatriot** in paragraph 2 refers to

   A. Metaphysics

   B. the planetary system

   C. Ptolemy

   D. an unformulated theory

4. Which of the sentences below is the best paraphrase of the following sentence from paragraph 4?

   While this finding, termed the Law of Universal Gravitation, is said to have been occasioned by Newton's observation of the fall of an apple from a tree in the orchard at his home, in reality, the idea did not come to the scientist in a flash of inspiration, but was developed slowly over time.

   A. Newton created his Law of Universal Gravitation immediately after he observed an apple falling from a tree in his orchard.

   B. The Law of Universal Gravitation, while similar on occasion to falling apples, is usually the result of observing objects which fall more slowly to earth.

   C. Newton's law of gravity was not the result of a single observation of a fruit tree, but rather was created over many years.

D. Stories about Newton's observance of falling apples are based on fact, rather than folklore, because of the time-consuming process of the theories relating to these stories.

5. The word **prescience** in the passage is closest in meaning to

   A. pre-scientific

   B. hindsight

   C. investigation

   D. perception

6. All of the following key facts about gravity are mentioned in paragraph 5 except:

   A. the effect of geology upon gravitational forces

   B. the impact of the varying density of the earth on gravity

   C. the manner in which gravitational force becomes weaker near the equator

   D. the way in which gravity influences rock formations

7. In paragraph 6, what is the author's main purpose?

   A. to emphasize the significance of Newton's achievement

   B. to identify a reservation which Newton experienced

C. to analyze natural phenomena

D. to reconcile various gravitational theories

8. Based on the information contained in paragraph 7, which of the following best explains the term "general relativity"?

A. changes in the motion of objects due to the curved path of space time

B. the inverse relationship between time and space

C. the proportionality between paths and objects

D. the manner in which later researchers supported Einstein

9. Look at the four stars { * } that indicate where the following sentence could be added to the passage:

Accordingly, an immense amount of research has been devoted to this subject throughout the twentieth and twenty-first centuries.

What is the correct position for this sentence?

A. {A*}

B. {B*}

C. {C*}

D. {D*}

10. According to paragraph 7, what can be inferred about the reaction of the scientific community to Einstein's theory of general relativity?

   A.   It has received a mixed response.

   B.   The response has been overwhelmingly positive.

   C.   The reception has been mostly negative.

   D.   The scientific community is still undecided about the value of Einstein's work.

11. According to the passage, what statement best describes Aristotle?

   A.   He was the founder of the Law of Universal Gravitation.

   B.   He was best-known for producing error-free work.

   C.   He was a famous Greek natural scientist.

   D.   He was a contemporary of Ptolemy.

12. Descartes is celebrated for establishing what subject?

   A.   mathematics

   B.   natural science

   C.   philosophy

   D.   physics

13. Select the group of three answers below that represents the most important ideas contained in the passage.

    A.   (i) Ptolemy is one of the most famous natural scientists.

            (ii) The strength of gravitational force is directly related to the distance to the equator.

            (iii) Newton was confused by the power from which gravity was derived.

    B.   (i) The study of the mechanics of motion has endured for many centuries.

            (ii) Ptolemy is one of the most famous natural scientists.

            (iii) Newton was confused by the power from which gravity was derived.

    C.   (i) The study of the mechanics of motion has endured for many centuries.

            (ii) Newton's study of gravitational forces was of invaluable significance.

            (iii) Einstein's theory of general relativity provided much-needed developments to Newton's work.

D. (i) Ptolemy is one of the most famous natural scientists.

(ii) The strength of gravitational force is directly related to the distance to the equator.

(iii) Einstein's theory of general relativity provided much-needed developments to Newton's work.

Reading Test Part 2:

Social Inequality

[1] Socio-economic status plays a key role in a child's success later in life, rather than intellectual ability, according to a recent study. As an example, let's direct our attention to two elementary school students named Paul and John. Both children are attentive and respectful to their teachers, and both earn good grades. However, Paul's father is an affluent property magnate, while John's dad works on an assembly line in a factory. Even though their academic aptitudes are similar, Paul is 30 times more likely than John to have a high-paying career before reaching his fortieth birthday simply due to the differences in the economic situations of their parents. Indeed, statistics reveal that students like John have a 12% chance of finding and keeping jobs that earn only median-level incomes. {A *}

[2] Research dealing with the economics of inequality among adults supports these findings. Importantly, these studies also reveal that the economics of inequality is a trend that has become more and more pronounced in recent years. For instance, in 1960, the **mean** after-tax pay for a U.S. corporate executive was more than 12 times that of the average factory worker. In 1974, the average CEO's pay had increased to nearly 35 times that of a typical blue-

collar worker. By 1980, the situation was even worse: the executive's wages and benefits were nearly 42 times that of the average wage of a factory worker. In the twenty-first century, this situation reached a level which some economists have called **hyper-inequality**. That is, it is now common for the salary of the average executive to be more than 100 times that of the average factory employee. In fact, in the current year, most CEOs are making, on average, 530 times more than blue-collar employees.

[3] Because of this and other economic dichotomies, a theoretical stance has recently sprung into existence, asserting that inequality is institutionalized. {B *} In keeping with this concept, many researchers argue that workers from higher socio-economic backgrounds are disproportionately compensated, even though the contribution they make to society is no more valuable than **that of their lower-paid counterparts**. To rectify the present imbalance caused by this economic **stratification**, researchers claim that economic rewards should be judged by and distributed according to the worthiness of the employment to society as a whole. Economic rewards under this schema refer not only to wages or salaries, but also to power, status, and prestige within one's community, as well as within larger society.

[4] Recently, cultural and critical theorists have joined in the economic debate that empirical researchers embarked upon decades ago. Focusing on the effect of cultural technologies and systems, they state that various forms of media promote the mechanisms of economic manipulation and oppression. Watching television, they claim, causes those of lower socio-economic class to view themselves as apolitical and powerless victims of the capitalistic machine. Of course, such a phenomenon would have a **deleterious** impact upon individual identity and human motivation. {C *}

[5] At a more personal level, economic inequality also has pervasive effects on the lives of the less economically fortunate. These personal effects include the manner in which one's economic status influences musical tastes, the perception of time and space, the expression of emotion, and the communication across social groups. The **detrimental** economic imbalance may at its most extreme form lead to differences in health and mortality in those from the lower economic levels of society. {D *}

[6] While causing problems to many on a personal level, economic inequality is also of concern from a global perspective. The worldwide impact of economic inequality is so severe at present that certain poorer countries are considered to be peripheral during discussions of international monetary policy. In order to solve this problem, many economists believe that consideration must be given not only to political arrangements that make some groups more financially better off than others, but also to the social interaction between people and groups.

[7] Conversely, other theorists argue that financial improvement does not always result in the betterment of any particular society. They point out that levels of personal happiness, as well as trust and cooperation between people, are often highest when monetary considerations within a group are kept to a minimum. Finally, they warn that judgements about any given nation's financial situation may be biased as a result of the Western emphasis on materialism and consumerism.

14. The word **mean** in the passage is closest in meaning to:

    A. unpleasant

    B. cheap

    C. basic

    D. average

15. Based on the information in paragraph 2, which of the following best explains the term **hyper-inequality**?

    A. The fact that the disparity between high and low level salaries has become so enormous.

    B. The fact that high and low level salaries are bifurcated.

    C. The fact that economists are keenly interested in the subject of financial inequality.

    D. The fact that CEOs have more prestige than factory workers.

16. The word **stratification** in the passage is closest in meaning to:

    A. paid at a low-level

    B. occurring in pairs

    C. divided into levels

    D. divided into steps of a process

17. The words **that of their lower-paid counterparts** in the passage refer to:

    A. the inequality which lower-paid workers encounter

    B. the compensation paid to people of lower-level incomes

    C. the salaries of people from affluent socio-economic strata

    D. the benefit to society from the work of lower compensated people

18. According to paragraph 4, all of the following are accurate statements except:

    A. Cultural theorists have expanded upon the work of previous research.

    B. Television and other media have an effect on social inequality.

    C. Television viewing can reinforce feelings of socio-economic subjugation.

    D. People who view television are more motivated to change their lives.

19. The word **detrimental** in the passage is closest in meaning to

    A. negative

    B. advantageous

    C. antisocial

    D. deathly

20. Look at the four stars { * } that indicate where the following sentence could be added to the passage.

    This burgeoning school of thought claims that social structures reinforce economic inequality by attaching more value and prestige to some careers than others.

    Where is the best place to insert this new sentence?

    A.   {A *}

    B.   {B *}

    C.   {C *}

    D.   {D *}

21. Which of the sentences below is the best paraphrase of the following sentence?

    The worldwide impact of economic inequality is so severe at present that certain poorer countries are considered to be peripheral during discussions of international monetary policy.

    A.   The influence of poverty has wide-reaching, global implications.

    B.   Some countries that are less economically advanced are thought to be irrelevant when debates about worldwide economic protocol take place.

C. Economic inequality has made certain countries poorer because of debates about international financial matters.

D. External discussions have increased the severity of worldwide financial inequality.

22. Why does the author mention Paul and John in paragraph 1 of the passage?

A. To emphasize the needs of blue-collar employees

B. To portray a tragic situation that has occurred in the past

C. To illustrate the economic effects of social inequality

D. To describe how poverty has impacted upon the life of one particular child

23. The word **deleterious** in the passage is closest in meaning to:

A. motivating

B. equalizing

C. injurious

D. judicious

24. According to the passage, which of the following statements best characterizes the personal effects of economic inequality?

   A. Socio-economic status has wide-ranging effects on life and lifestyle, as well as on a number of personal preferences and behaviors.

   B. Socio-economic level primarily affects communication skills.

   C. Socio-economic unfairness results predominantly in lethargy among those most profoundly affected by it.

   D. Socio-economic inequality usually results in premature death to those who experience it.

25. According to paragraph 6 of the passage, how might the global effects of economic inequality be solved?

   A. by focusing on international political discussions on this problem

   B. by paying attention to the political as well as the social causes of inequality

   C. by heeding the results of various social interactions

   D. by exploring the way in which the political and social aspects of inequality are intertwined

26. Based on the information in paragraph 7, what can be inferred about the present debate on socio-economic inequality?

    A. All theorists agree about the best course of action to take in order to address the issue of economic disparities.

    B. There is unanimous agreement that an improvement in financial conditions leads to an amelioration of other social problems.

    C. There is some dispute surrounding the social and non-monetary effects associated with financial improvement.

    D. Western capitalism serves as the agreed upon, uniform standard towards which all nations should strive.

Reading Test Part 3:

Mount Rushmore

[1] In the Black Hills in the state of South Dakota in the United States, four **visages** protrude from the side of a mountain. The faces are those of four United States' presidents: George Washington, Thomas Jefferson, Theodore Roosevelt, and Abraham Lincoln. Overseen and directed by the Danish-American sculptor John Gutzon Borglum, the work on this giant display of outdoor art was a Herculean task that took 14 years to complete. {A *}

[2] A South Dakota state historian named Doane Robinson originally conceived of the idea for the memorial sculpture. He proposed that the work be dedicated to popular figures who were prominent in the western United States and accordingly suggested statues of western heroes such as Buffalo Bill Cody and Kit Carson. Deeming a project dedicated to popular heroes **frivolous**, Borglum rejected Robinson's proposal. It was Borglum's firm conviction that the mountain carving be used to memorialize individuals of national, rather than regional, importance. {B *}

[3] Mount Rushmore therefore became a national memorial, dedicated to the four presidents who were considered most pivotal in US history. Washington was

chosen on the basis of being the first president. Jefferson, who was of course a president, was also instrumental in the writing of the American Declaration of Independence. Lincoln was selected on the basis of the mettle he demonstrated during the American Civil war, and Roosevelt for his development of the Square Deal policy, as well as being a proponent of the construction of the Panama Canal. Commencing with Washington's head first, Borglum quickly realized that it would be best to work on only one head at a time, in order to make it compatible with its surroundings. In order to help him visualize the **final outcome**, he fashioned a 1.5 meter high plaster model on a scale of 1 to 12.

[4] Work on the venture began in 1927 and was completed in 1941. The cost of the project was nearly $1,000,000, which was raised mostly from national government funds, and also from charitable donations from magnanimous and benevolent members of the public. The carving of the mountain was tedious and arduous work, employing 360 men who worked in groups of 30. {C *} The daily working conditions on the mountainside can best be described as treacherous. For instance, men were often strapped inside leather harnesses that dangled over the cliff edge. Further, workers needed great strength to withstand the exertion of drilling into the mountainside.

[5] The workmen faced frequent delays due to a dearth of financial backing in the early days, in addition to inclement weather throughout the 14 year period. Adverse conditions were also discovered when the carving of Jefferson began. The detection of poor quality stone on the mountain to the left of Washington resulted in Jefferson's face being repositioned to the right side. In spite of these setbacks, Mount Rushmore remained the best choice for the **venue** of the memorial. {D *} Yet, a large amount of the rock had to be blasted away from the mountain using dynamite or pneumatic drills, and as a result, approximately 450,000 tons of rock still lies at the foot of the mountain today.

[6] Each of the four heads on the mountaintop is approximately 18 meters in height. Each nose is roughly six meters in length, while each mouth is approximately five meters wide. Needless to say, creating facial expressions on such an immense scale was not child's play. It required the work of a true craftsman like Borglum to give each face its own unique character. In particular, Borglum's attention to detail on the eyes of each president was a stroke of genius. He gave the eyes a lifelike quality by making each pupil hollow in order to reflect the natural sunlight.

[7] Sadly, Borglum passed away in March of 1941, just months prior to the completion of the presidential memorial. In loving memory of his father, Lincoln Borglum, the son of John Gutzon Borglum, carried the project to completion. Having labored on the mountain as an adolescent, Lincoln was aptly-qualified to supervise the finishing touches on this mammoth monument.

27. The word **visages** in this passage is closest in meaning to:

    A. bodies

    B. noses

    C. heads

    D. faces

28. The word **frivolous** in this passage is closest in meaning to:

    A. unimportant

    B. serious

    C. expensive

    D. unwanted

29. The words **final outcome** in this passage refer to:

    A. the completion of Washington's head

    B. the rendering of the plaster model

C. the finished sculpture of all four presidents

D. the process of making Washington's face fit in with the others

30. According to the passage, all of the following statements about Mount Rushmore are true except:

   A. The project was predominantly funded on a federal level.

   B. Generous private individuals contributed financial backing for the work.

   C. Funding was plentiful at the beginning of the project.

   D. Adverse weather conditions sometimes hampered work on the project.

31. Look at the four stars { * } that indicate where the following sentence could be added to the passage.

   The mountain consists of granite, a fine-grained stone that is amenable to cutting and carving.

   Where is the best place to insert this new sentence?

   A. {A *}

   B. {B *}

   C. {C *}

   D. {D *}

32. The word **venue** in this passage is closest in meaning to:

   A. rock

   B. mountain

   C. site

   D. consideration

33. Why did Doane Robinson suggest that western heroes be the subject of the monument?

   A. Western heroes were well-known and loved by the public.

   B. The westward expansion movement would not have been successful without Buffalo Bill Cody and Kit Carson.

   C. Such figures were of national importance.

   D. The dedication of a sculpture to Western heroes would raise their profiles.

34. Based solely on the information contained in paragraphs 2 and 3 of the passage, which of the following statements best describes the selection of presidents for Mount Rushmore?

   A. There was some debate about which presidents to choose.

   B. These four presidents were well known internationally.

C. These presidents changed the course of US policy and history.

D. These presidents were of some importance regionally.

35. Why was it necessary to change the location of the carving for Jefferson?

    A. because of poor weather

    B. due to a lack of money

    C. because the rock on the original location was of inferior condition

    D. since Borglum changed his mind

36. In paragraph 6, the author provides the specific measurements of the features of Mount Rushmore in order to:

    A. reveal that the carving lacks a sense of artistic proportion.

    B. underscore the imposing and impressive size of the monument.

    C. emphasize the importance of continuous financing for the work.

    D. criticize the amount of money spent on the sculpture.

37. Based solely on the information contained in paragraph 7, what can be inferred about the work of Lincoln Borglum?

    A. It meant that the project was completed on time.

    B. The project was behind schedule when his father died.

C. He worked begrudgingly on the project as a teenager.

D. He completed the monument competently as a tribute to his father.

38. Which of the following statements accurately expresses the author's attitude about John Gutzon Borglum and his work?

   A. He was a talented and perceptive artist.

   B. He was profligate in his spending for the Mount Rushmore project.

   C. His work was misunderstood during his lifetime.

   D. He was an incompetent mentor for his son.

39. Summarize the passage by selecting the group of sentences below that express the most important ideas contained in the passage:

   A. (i) Mount Rushmore was dedicated to presidents of crucial importance.

   (ii) The Mount Rushmore project was beset with various difficulties.

   (iii) Members of the public donated money towards the project.

   B. (i) Mount Rushmore was dedicated to presidents of crucial importance.

   (ii) The Mount Rushmore project was beset with various difficulties.

   (iii) The project was a large-scale, time-consuming, and dangerous task.

C. (i) Members of the public donated money towards the project.

   (ii) The project was a large-scale, time-consuming, and dangerous task.

   (iii) The eyes of each face on the memorial are vivid and lifelike.

D. (i) The project was a large-scale, time-consuming, and dangerous task.

   (ii) The eyes of each face on the memorial are vivid and lifelike.

   (iii) Lincoln Borglum completed the Mount Rushmore project.

40. The passage you have read discusses the construction of the Mount Rushmore project. Which of the following helped John Gutzon Borglum achieve an artistic, yet realistic-looking result?

   A. (i) receiving sufficient funding

      (ii) building the scale model

   B. (i) receiving sufficient funding

      (ii) paying attention to detail

   C. (i) building the scale model

      (ii) paying attention to detail

   D. (i) paying attention to detail

      (ii) devoting the memorial to national figures

TOEFL Practice Reading – Test 2
Answer Key

1. B
2. A
3. C
4. C
5. D
6. D
7. B
8. A
9. D
10. B
11. C
12. A
13. C
14. D
15. A
16. C
17. D
18. D
19. A
20. B

21. B
22. C
23. C
24. A
25. B
26. C
27. D
28. A
29. C
30. C
31. D
32. C
33. A
34. C
35. C
36. B
37. D
38. A
39. B
40. C

TOEFL Practice Reading – Test 2 Answers and Explanations

1) The correct answer is B. Notice that the word "renowned" is from the root word "known."

2) The correct answer is A. The theory described in paragraph 2 appeared in the first century. It is also described as "unformulated." For these reasons, we know that the theory was newly formed.

3) The correct answer is C. "Compatriot" means a person who has the same nationality as someone else. At the beginning of paragraph 2, Ptolemy is described as "another Greek scientist."

4) The correct answer is C. "Flash of inspiration" means that a single event caused a positive outcome. It is the opposite of the phrase "slowly developed over time." So, the law of gravity was created slowly.

5) The correct answer is D. The phrase "Newton must also be acknowledged for the realization that . . ." at the end of paragraph 5 emphasizes Newton's "prescience" or "realization."

6) The correct answer is D. Paragraph 5 mentions "geological features" so we know that A is true. Paragraph 5 also mentions "the declining mass and density of the planet from the equator" so we know that B is also true. Finally, Paragraph

5 mentions that "gravity becomes less robust [or less strong] as the distance from the equator diminishes" so we know that C is true. D is incorrect because gravity influences rocks and geological features. The rocks do not influence gravity.

7) The correct answer is B. "Reservation" means confusion or doubt. It is close in meaning to the word "perplexed" and the phrase "unable adequately to explain."

8) The correct answer is A. Paragraph 7 states that "Einstein asserted that the paths of objects in motion can sometimes . . . change direction . . . as a result of the curvature of space time."

9) The correct answer is D. Paragraph 6 concludes by describing these hypotheses today. So, we must be speaking about the twenty-first century as mentioned in the new sentence.

10) The correct answer is B. Paragraph 7 states that Einstein's work was "revolutionary" and that it has been "unequivocally supported." Both of these statements describe positive reactions.

11) The correct answer is C. Paragraph 1 describes Aristotle as a "Greek philosopher and natural scientist." A is false because Newton discovered gravity. B is false because this idea is not mentioned in the passage. D is false because Ptolemy lived four centuries after Aristotle.

12) The correct answer is A. Paragraph 3 states that "Descartes [. . .] was later dubbed [or named] the father of modern mathematics . . ."

13) The correct answer is C. These are the three main ideas. The other items give specific details.

14) The correct answer is D. Notice that the word "average" is used five times in paragraph two. Look for word repetition like this as you try to find synonyms on the reading test.

15) The correct answer is A. "Disparity" means difference. "Enormous" means very large. So, the statistics given in paragraph 2 support statement A.

16) The correct answer is C. The passage uses words like "bifurcate" and "dichotomy" to talk about the division of the economy. The passage also talks about high and low levels of salary.

17) The correct answer is D. The grammatical subject of this clause in the sentence is "contribution." "Benefit" and "contribution" are near synonyms.

18) The correct answer is D. Paragraph 4 states that "Recently, cultural and critical theorists have joined in the economic debate", so A is correct. Paragraph 4 also states that "various forms of media promote the mechanisms of economic manipulation and oppression", so B is correct. Finally, paragraph 4 states that

"those of lower socio-economic class . . . view themselves as . . . powerless victims." So C is also correct.

19) The correct answer is A. The entire passage speaks about the negative effects of the present economic situation.

20) The correct answer is B. The phrase "a theoretical stance has recently sprung into existence" in paragraph 3 is similar in meaning to the phrase "burgeoning school of thought" in the new sentence above.

21) The correct answer is B. "Poorer countries" is synonymous with "less economically advanced." "Peripheral" is similar in meaning to "irrelevant." Finally, "policy" is similar in meaning to "protocol."

22) The correct answer is C. The economic effects of social inequality is the main theme of this reading passage. So, the author wants to illustrate the main theme. The answers B and D are too strongly-worded and emphatic, and answer A is too specific.

23) The correct answer is C. The passage is speaking about the harm caused to low-paid people. Answers A, B, and D contain words with positive connotations.

24) The correct answer is A. This is the main idea from paragraph 4. Note that answer choice D exaggerates the consequence of early death.

25) The correct answer is B. Paragraph 6 states: "In order to solve this problem, many economists believe that consideration must be given not only to political arrangements . . . but also to the social interaction between people and groups." Answers A and C are incorrect because the paragraph describes both of these problems. Answer D is incorrect because the paragraph does not discuss the interaction between the political and social aspects.

26) The correct answer is C. The word "conversely" at the beginning of paragraph 7 indicates that there is a dispute or disagreement.

27) The correct answer is D. The next sentence begins "The faces." So "face" and "visage" are synonyms.

28) The correct answer is A. Paragraph 2 states that the figures were of "national . . . importance", instead of merely "popular." So "frivolous" and "unimportant" are synonyms.

29) The correct answer is C. A "scale model" is a replica of a complete finished project. This idea is mentioned at the end of paragraph 3.

30) The correct answer is C. Paragraph 5 states that there was "a dearth of financial backing in the early days" of the project. "Dearth" means lack.

31) The correct answer is D. The sentences in paragraph 5 before and after {D *} describe the mountain. Since the new sentence mentions a specific characteristic of the mountain, it fits best in paragraph 5.

32) The correct answer is C. The memorial is located on the mountain, which is described in paragraph 5. Location, venue, and site are synonyms.

33) The correct answer is A. Paragraph 2 states that the western heroes were "popular." This means that they received the public's admiration.

34) The correct answer is C. The beginning of paragraph 3 states: "Mount Rushmore therefore became a national memorial, dedicated to the four presidents who were considered most pivotal in US history." "Pivotal" means very important or significant.

35) The correct answer is C. Paragraph 5 states: "The detection of poor quality stone on the mountain to the left of Washington resulted in Jefferson's face being repositioned to the right side."

36) The correct answer is B. Paragraph 6 states that "creating facial expressions on such an immense scale was not child's play."

37) The correct answer is D. Paragraph 7 states that "Lincoln was aptly-qualified to supervise the finishing touches on this mammoth monument." "Aptly-qualified" means competent.

38) The correct answer is A. Paragraph 6 describes the artist as "a true craftsman" and a "genius."

39) The correct answer is B. These three statements state the main ideas of the passage. The other statements contain specific ideas.

40) The correct answer is C. These two statements give the reasons for Borglum's artistic achievement. The other statements are true, but they do not pertain to the artistic aspect of the project.

TOEFL iBT Reading Comprehension – Practice Test 3

Instructions: The reading test contains 3 parts (38 total questions). You have 60 minutes to complete all three parts of the reading test.

Reading Test Part 1:

Tourism

[1] Adventurers, fieldwork assistants, and volunteers are gradually replacing tourists. Still, the classification 'tourist' will never totally disappear. There might still be those who wish to travel to foreign lands for their own enjoyment, but doing so will be a **clandestine** and frowned-upon activity. No one will admit to belonging to that category.

[2] Burma and Bali have recently prohibited tourists from entering parts of their countries. The list of places that tourists cannot explore is ever-expanding. The international tourist organization Tourism Concern states that Belize, Botswana, China, East Africa, Peru, Thailand, and Zanzibar all have areas that have been adversely impacted upon by tourism. Representatives from the organization Tourism Concern believe that tourists are destroying the environment, as well as local cultures. These representatives also assert that although tourists bring money to the countries they visit, they must be stopped at any price. {A *}

[3] **These notions** may seem ironic since tourism was unquestionably encouraged as something that was inherently good a few decades ago. The advent of relatively less expensive accommodation and flights has meant that tourism can finally be enjoyed by the majority of the population. The United Nations declared the year 1967 "The International Year of the Tourist," and at the beginning of the twenty-first century, more and more families are traveling abroad on family vacations. {B *}

[4] The World Tourism Organization (WTO) has predicted that by the year 2050, there will be 1.56 billion tourists per year traveling somewhere in the world. This forecast demonstrates the immense challenge in trying to curb the global demand for tourism. In fact, the task may be so tremendous that it might just be impossible.

[5] Some argue that the government should intervene, but the government alone would face huge impediments in attempting to make so many economically-empowered people stop doing something that they enjoy. Others assert that

tourism is of such extreme damage to the welfare of the world that only totally irresponsible individuals would ever consider doing it. Yet, this argument is clearly **absurd**. Whatever benefits or otherwise accrue from tourism, it is not evil, despite what a tiny minority might say. It can cause harm. It can be neutral, and it can occasionally bring about something good.

[6] As a result, tourism is under attack by more a more oblique method: it has been re-named. Bit by bit, the word "tourist" is being removed from the tourism industry.

[7] Since tourism has changed, so too must the vacation. Adventurers, fieldwork assistants, and volunteers do not go on vacations. These new travelers go on "cultural experiences", "expeditions" or "projects". However, re-branding tourism in this way gives freedom to travelers, as well as restrictions.

[8] The various booklets, pamphlets, and brochures distributed by the new industry for travelers are now attempting to **emulate** advertisements produced by charities. For example, *Global Adventure* magazine produces an annual "99 Great Adventures Guide" which mixes charitable expeditions with vacations as if the two things are one and the same.

[9] New travelers express great interest in respecting the environments they visit. They avoid **tourist infrastructures** because they are afraid of being viewed negatively by the local culture. Instead, they prefer accommodation arrangements such as cabins or camping. These types of accommodation, they believe, are more respectful of local culture. Local culture is very important to the new tourist, whereas the mass tourist is believed to destroy it. {C *}

[10] Nevertheless, all types of tourism should be responsible towards and respectful of environmental and human resources. Some tourism developers, as well as individual tourists, have not acted with this in mind. Consequently, a divide is being driven between those few **affluent** and privileged tourists and the remaining majority. {D *}

1. What is the best title for this passage?
    A. Tourism and the Environment
    B. Adventurers, Tourists, and Travelers
    C. The Changing Face of Tourism
    D. Tourism: Its Advantages and Disadvantages

2. The word **clandestine** in the passage is closest in meaning to:

   A. distressing

   B. secret

   C. pleasurable

   D. difficult

3. The author mentions all off the following facts about tourism in paragraphs 2 and 3 except:

   A. The names of certain countries that have banned tourists.

   B. The names of countries that have been negatively affected by tourism.

   C. The reasons why flights became inexpensive.

   D. The reasons why new views on tourism may seem paradoxical when compared to views on tourism in the past.

4. The word **absurd** in the passage is closest in meaning to:

   A. ridiculous

   B. beneficial

   C. proper

   D. damaging

5. The word **emulate** in the passage is closest in meaning to:

   A. strive

   B. utilize

   C. imitate

   D. distribute

6. Look at the four stars { * } that indicate where the following sentence could be added to the passage.

   Our concern should be not with this small number of privileged people, but rather with the majority of travelers.

   Where is the best place to insert this new sentence?

   A. {A *}

   B. {B *}

   C. {C *}

   D. {D *}

7. Which of the sentences below is the best paraphrase of the following sentence from paragraph 5?

   Whatever benefits or otherwise accrue from tourism, it is not evil, despite what a tiny minority might say.

A. Although the benefits of tourism may be questionable, tourism is not morally wrong, in spite of what a few detractors might believe.

B. Even though some people may believe tourism is wicked, it is not really wrong because of its obvious benefits.

C. Tourism should not be stopped, in spite of some disadvantages, because it may be beneficial to the minority.

D. In spite of what a few people believe, very few benefits result from tourism.

8. Based on the information in paragraph 9, which of the following best explains the term **tourist infrastructures**?

A. Hotels and other physical structures that have been purpose-built for tourists.

B. New campgrounds and cabins that have been erected for tourists.

C. Buildings and other physical structures that show respect for the local environment.

D. Any structure that lessens the divide between tourism and the local culture.

9. The words **these notions** in the passage refer to:

   A. The way that tourists bring money to the countries they visit.

   B. The manner in which tourism helps local cultures.

   C. The fact that tourism used to be encouraged as something good.

   D. The viewpoints that express disdain for tourism.

10. Why does the author mention "cultural experiences," "expeditions" or "projects" in paragraph 7 of the passage?

    A. To exemplify how tourists respect the environment

    B. To contradict the evidence in support of advertising

    C. To illustrate how tourism has been re-branded

    D. To argue that charitable expeditions are now indistinguishable from vacations

11. According to the passage, which of the following examples best characterizes how tourists can be more respectful of their environments?

    A. By avoiding the local culture

    B. By using unconventional types of lodging arrangements

    C. By viewing the local culture in a negative way

    D. By emphasizing the disadvantages of mass tourism

12. The word **affluent** in the passage is closest in meaning to:

    A.   obnoxious

    B.   detrimental

    C.   oblivious

    D.   wealthy

13. Which of the following best expresses the author's attitude towards the past effects of tourism on the environment?

    A.   regrettable

    B.   capricious

    C.   unclear

    D.   uncertain

Reading Test Part 2:

Sickly Youth

[1] Every morning, tens of thousands of children under age ten have nothing to eat or drink before leaving home for school. Research also shows that out of all youths in the 13-year-old age group, 7% are regular smokers. In addition, the consumption of alcoholic beverages in the 11-to-15-year-old age group has more than doubled in the past decade, with 25% of this age group drinking on average the equivalent of over four cans of beer every week.

[2] In spite of an overall trend for improvements in child health, inequalities in health have been on the rise. A significant aspect of **health inequalities** is that rates of disease and death are far higher in poorer households. One key reason for **tackling** the issue of child poverty is to rectify in particular the inequalities in child health, which will otherwise carry over into adulthood. Accordingly, the government has made the commitment to attempt to lower child poverty dramatically in the next two decades. {A *}

[3] But will the government's commitment actually reduce child poverty and improve child health? **Cynics** say that the government's monetary support for poor households will invariably be spent on consumables like candy and potato chips, or other junk food, or worse, on tobacco, alcohol, and even drugs. {B *} Realistically, however, providing households with more money in the form of governmental assistance should give them the opportunity to spend more money on nutritious, often more expensive, food.

[4] Yet, if the government truly wishes to improve the health of poor children, it should realize that families cannot rely on only modest increases in income. For the children leaving home without any breakfast, these government measures are not enough. A better option would be to feed **these children** through school breakfast and dinner programs. {C *}

[5] In fact, research demonstrates that children's concentration and learning suffer when they do not have a nutritious breakfast. In response to this research, some countries have developed programs for nutritious school breakfasts and dinners, and **they** have allocated more funds to these meal programs than to welfare benefits. {D *} There remains a clear need for the authorities to address nutrition as one of the worst symptoms of child poverty since disadvantaged children in many areas still do not get a nourishing breakfast and the effectiveness of their education is jeopardized as a result.

[6] Smoking also greatly damages the health of children and increases childhood mortality rates. While the government has raised the cigarette tax, thereby increasing the cost of tobacco to consumers, this has not brought about the desired result. On the contrary, it has left poor parents who smoke worse off, and their children will continue to suffer. Children's health would be better served if the government allocated funds to preventing cigarette sales to children, instead of the hefty monetary resources spent on attempting to halt cigarette smuggling and related tax evasion.

[7] Children, particularly young adolescents, are also sickly because of the ever-increasing consumption of alcohol in this age group. One reason for the rise in children's drinking is the increase in the availability of sweetened bottled alcoholic drinks like wine coolers. These beverages make alcohol more attractive and more **palatable** to young people and children. Nevertheless, the government appears be in something of a quandary, perhaps wishing to speak out against major beverage manufacturing companies, and yet succumbing to lobbying by and accepting related financial support from big businesses like Anheuser-Busch.

[8] Improving children's opportunities depends on ending child poverty and improving the health of the poorest children. While these goals are related, it would be foolish to believe that the reduction of child poverty would automatically improve children's nutrition and reduce their smoking and drinking. Re-thinking the allocation of governmental funds to nutrition and effective education and prevention about addiction are still needed in order to improve child health.

14. According to paragraph 1, the following statements are true except:

    A. Many young children regularly go to school on an empty stomach.

    B. Alcohol consumption has risen across many age groups in the last ten years.

    C. Children as young as thirteen years old have developed smoking habits.

    D. Twenty-five percent of a certain age group regularly consumes alcohol every week.

15. The best definition for the word **tackling** in the passage is:

    A. trying to solve

    B. attempting to analyze

    C. understanding the trends

    D. committing to change

16. Based upon paragraph 2, which is the best explanation of the term **health inequalities**?

    A. Poor children are often hungry and undernourished.

    B. There has been an increased trend for improvements in child health.

    C. Mortality and illness rates are greater for members of poor families.

    D. The government has made a commitment to solve the problems of the poorest children.

17. The best synonym for the word **cynics** in the passage is:

    A. officials

    B. consumers

    C. advisers

    D. doubters

18. Look at the four stars { * } that indicate where the following sentence could be added to the passage.

    Giving free school meals to children from lower-income families would be the best and most direct way of improving child nutrition.

    Where is the best place to insert this new sentence?

    A. {A *}

B. {B *}

C. {C *}

D. {D *}

19. The word **they** highlighted in paragraph 5 refers to:

    A. countries that have established school breakfasts.

    B. children who regularly do not receive breakfast.

    C. researchers in the field of child nutrition.

    D. fund-raisers for school meal programs.

20. Which of the sentences below is the best paraphrase of the following sentence from paragraph 5?

    There remains a clear need for the authorities to address nutrition as one of the worst symptoms of child poverty since disadvantaged children in many areas still do not get a nourishing breakfast and the effectiveness of their education is jeopardized as a result.

    A. The government needs to provide nourishing breakfasts to children so that they can improve their learning.

    B. Poor children do not start the day with a good meal and cannot learn well as a result, so it is of the utmost importance for the government to improve child poverty and child nutrition.

C. Child poverty continues to be a grave social problem and nutrition is a concomitant issue; therefore, the government should get involved.

D. Poor nutrition is one aspect of poverty and increased government funds need to be set aside to deal with this situation.

21. Why does the author discuss smoking in paragraph 6 of the passage?

   A. To establish the link between cigarette smuggling and tax evasion

   B. To exemplify how poor parents who smoke will continue to do so, exacerbating their children's health problems

   C. To enumerate details about a government policy

   D. To expand on another aspect of poor health in children

22. According to the passage, what was the main reason for the government's increase in the cigarette tax?

   A. To reduce childhood death rates

   B. To decrease tax evasion relating to tobacco products

   C. To attempt to deter smoking, particularly by poor parents

   D. To impede cigarette smuggling

23. The best synonym for the word **palatable** in the passage is:

   A. acceptable

   B. tasty

   C. desirable

   D. pleasant

24. Based on the information in paragraph 7, what can be inferred about the government's reluctance to criticize the practices of big businesses?

   A. It is loath to lose the monetary support that large beverage companies have to offer.

   B. It realizes that there is no reason to reduce the demand for certain alcoholic drinks.

   C. It wishes to reduce its reliance on financing from lobbyists.

   D. It understands that doing so would not make alcohol less attractive to youngsters.

25. Based on the information in paragraph 8, which statement best describes the relationship between the goals of improved opportunities for children and the problems of child poverty and ill health?

   A. The reduction of governmental reliance on large companies is inextricably intertwined with the goal of improving children's opportunities.

   B. The government needs to re-evaluate its relationship to lobbyists if it is ever going to solve the issue of poor child health.

   C. Establishing the goal of addressing of child poverty will dramatically improve children's health and opportunities, but it may take an extended time period to do so.

   D. The achievement of the goal of the reduction of child poverty would improve child health and increase the opportunities of children to some extent, but it would not entirely eradicate the problem.

26. What is the author's main purpose in this passage?

   A. To decry poor child health and point the finger at the primary culprits

   B. To demonstrate that child health would automatically improve if certain solutions were to be carried out

C. To enumerate the reasons for health inequalities, particularly in children, and to allude to some possible courses of action

D. To demonstrate the reasons why the consumption of alcohol and tobacco are harmful for children

Reading Test Part 3:

Social Trends

[1] Results of a survey on social trends have identified a rise in immigration as the most significant social change in recent years. Homegrown population increases, defined as the surplus of births over deaths, have been surpassed by immigration. In other words, immigration has increased, while natural population growth has fallen. Specifically, at the end of the twentieth century, net inward migration increased, while natural population growth fell. This amounted to a shift in the significance of immigration to changes in the population, with consequences for ethnic mix and structure. Population patterns have changed dramatically as immigration has become the main **catalyst** for population growth. Moreover, migration patterns within the country appear to be closely linked to where and how people choose to live.

[2] In spite of **this steady influx** of new members of the population, most people regard immigration as a very good thing which benefits the country. These benefits include the skills brought by workers that are needed to expand the information technology industry. The younger age profile of immigrants also helps to balance the pressures of an aging population. {A *}

[3] The survey also revealed other important social trends relating to immigration and population. Notably, the population tripled from almost 76 million at the beginning of the twentieth century to nearly 281 million at the start of the twenty-first century. {B *} Average household size declined by 2 people per household over the last century, from 4.6 people per household a hundred years ago to 2.6 members per household today. Population density has increased two-fold during the last one hundred years, but remains relatively low in comparison to most other countries in the world. Alaska had the lowest population density, and the population density of the Northeast, which has always been high, continued consistently to **outstrip** that of other regional areas. While most of the population lived outside cities prior to the end of World War II, the percentage of the population living in metropolitan areas increased in every subsequent decade of the study. New York and California had the largest populations, and Florida and Arizona had the fastest-growing populations during the period of the study. {C *}

[4] Until 1970, the majority of households were living in the Northeast and Midwest, but since 1980 the majority was in the South and West. Slightly more than half of all households are now maintained by people aged 45 and over. Female householders have increased as a proportion of all householders, and older females were far more likely to live alone than were men or younger women. {D *} The per capita marriage rate has fallen in the last fifteen years, and there was a concurrent drop in the per capita divorce rate during this time.

[5] The survey also examined changes to overall national income, as well as the spending habits of individuals and households. It has found that the distribution of income has become more and more unequal over the past forty years, with the income of the richest 10% of the people in the country rising disproportionately to that of the poorest sector of the population. As relatively worse-off households struggle to make essential purchases, the amount of consumer credit has recently increased to over a trillion dollars, with credit cards and revolving credit arrangements constituting the **lion's share of** this figure. Cash transactions fell sharply as innovative technologies and new forms of payment appeared in the marketplace.

27. The word **catalyst** in this passage is closest in meaning to:

   A. resource

   B. reference

   C. reason

   D. result

28. The words **this steady influx** in this passage refer to:

    A.   the consistent improvement in ethnic diversity in the population.

    B.   the constant increase in people coming to the country for the first time.

    C.   the continual stream of benefits and skills brought by new workers.

    D.   the gradual expansion in the technology sector.

29. According to paragraph 3, what was the most notable change to the population in the last one hundred years?

    A.   The three-fold increase in the size of the population

    B.   The increase in average household size

    C.   The worryingly high rise in population density

    D.   The low population density in Alaska

30. Look at the four stars { * } that indicate where the following sentence could be added to the passage.

    There was also a dramatic decline in the number of households with 5 or more members and a significant increase the number of one and two-person households.

    Where is the best place to insert this new sentence?

    A.   {A *}

    B.   {B *}

C. {C *}

D. {D *}

31. The word **outstrip** in this passage is closest in meaning to:

    A. overwhelm

    B. compare to

    C. diminish

    D. exceed

32. Why does the author mention the changes to the populations of Florida and Arizona?

    A. To point out that new residents are continually moving to these states

    B. To contrast their population changes to those in New York and California

    C. To exemplify the increase in the percentage of the population living in metropolitan areas

    D. To illustrate why people wish to leave the Northeast and Midwest

33. The phrase **lion's share of** in this passage is closest in meaning to:

   A. background to

   B. indebtedness to

   C. majority of

   D. fluctuating part of

34. Which of the following statements expresses a possible interpretation of the relationship between the changes to the marriage rate and divorce rate?

   A. The marriage rate went down because more women preferred to live alone.

   B. The divorce rate went down because fewer people got married during the period of the study.

   C. The marriage rated went down because the core of the population is aging.

   D. The divorce rate declined because existing marriages became more stable.

35. According to paragraph 4, the most notable demographic shift when comparing geographic areas was that:

   A. Female householders rose as a percentage of all householders.

   B. Older females live alone more often than do men or younger women.

   C. The population rose sharply in California and New York over the course of the study.

   D. Many people moved from the Northeast and Midwest to live in the South or West.

36. Based on the information contained in the passage, what could be inferred about the reason why female householders increased as a proportion of all householders?

   A. Women are preoccupied about the needs of their children, so they deprioritize other relationships.

   B. Women generally suffer from a decline in household income after the breakup of a relationship.

   C. Women are more likely to live alone after losing a life partner than men are.

   D. The social stigma of divorce is greater for women than men.

37. According to the passage, there has been a surge in consumer credit due to:

   A.   the reliance upon the use of credit cards to make purchases.

   B.   the unequal distribution of income in the general population.

   C.   the spending habits of the richest sector of the population.

   D.   the fall in cash transactions as a result of new technologies.

38. Summarize the passage by selecting the group of sentences below that express the three most important ideas contained in the passage:

   A.   (i) The population has increased as a result of immigration.

   (ii) There were notable changes in the concentration of the population in certain states and geographic regions.

   (iii) The distribution of income has become increasingly skewed in favor of the rich.

   B.   (i) The population has increased due to increased birth rates and rising immigration.

   (ii) There were notable changes in the concentration of the population in certain states and geographic regions.

(iii) The distribution of income has become increasingly skewed in favor of the rich.

C.   (i) There were notable changes in the concentration of the population in certain states and geographic regions.

(ii) Marriage and divorce rates have fallen.

(iii) The distribution of income has become increasingly skewed in favor of the rich.

D.   (i) There were notable changes in the concentration of the population in certain states and geographic regions.

(ii) The distribution of income has become increasingly skewed in favor of the rich.

(iii) More and more women prefer to live alone.

TOEFL Practice Reading – Test 3
Answer Key

1. C
2. B
3. C
4. A
5. C
6. D
7. A
8. A
9. D
10. C
11. B
12. D
13. A
14. B
15. A
16. C
17. D
18. C
19. A
20. B
21. D
22. C
23. B
24. A
25. D
26. C
27. C
28. B
29. A
30. B
31. D
32. A
33. C
34. B
35. D
36. C
37. A
38. A

TOEFL Practice Reading – Test 3 Answers and Explanations

1) The correct answer is C. The best title for the passage is "The Changing Face of Tourism." The first sentence of the passage states: "Adventurers, fieldwork assistants, and volunteers are gradually replacing tourists." This sentence introduces the idea of changes to tourism, and these changes are explained in depth in the passage.

2) The correct answer is B. The word "clandestine" has the same meaning as "secret." We know that tourism has become a secret activity because paragraph 1 states that traveling for enjoyment has become a "frowned-upon activity [. . . that] no one will admit to."

3) The correct answer is C. The author does not discuss the reasons why flights became inexpensive. The passage merely states that "the advent of relatively less expensive accommodation and flights has meant that tourism can finally be enjoyed by the majority."

4) The correct answer is A. "Absurd" means ridiculous. The author states that there would be "impediments in attempting to make so many economically-empowered people stop doing something they enjoy" so we know that the author disagrees with the previous assertions in paragraph 5.

5) The correct answer is C. "Emulate" means to imitate. The example in paragraph 8 points out that *Global Adventure* magazine treats charitable expeditions and vacations "as if the two things are one and the same."

6) The correct answer is D. The best place to insert this new sentence is at the end of the passage. The new sentence says that "Our concern should be not with this small number of privileged people, but rather with the majority of travelers." The phrase "this small number of privileged people" refers to the "few affluent and privileged tourists" mentioned at the end of the passage.

7) The correct answer is A. The best paraphrase of the sentence "Whatever benefits or otherwise accrue from tourism, it is not evil, despite what a tiny minority might say" is as follows: "Although the benefits of tourism may be questionable, tourism is not morally wrong, in spite of what a few detractors might believe." The phrase "although the benefits of tourism may be questionable" has the same meaning as "whatever benefits or otherwise accrue from tourism, it is not evil," and the phrase "what a few detractors might believe" has the same meaning as "what a tiny minority might say."

8) The correct answer is A. The phrase "tourist infrastructures" refers to hotels and other physical structures that have been purpose-built for tourists. We know this because the next sentence in paragraph 9 talks about accommodation.

9) The correct answer is D. The words "these notions" refer to the viewpoints that express disdain for tourism. We know this because the previous sentence in the passage expresses the belief that tourism "must be stopped at any price."

10) The correct answer is C. The author mentions "cultural experiences", "expeditions" or "projects" in paragraph 7 of the passage to illustrate how tourism has been re-branded. The last sentence of paragraph 7 states that "re-branding tourism in this way gives freedom to travelers, as well as restrictions."

11) The correct answer is B. Using unconventional types of lodging arrangements characterizes how tourists can be more respectful of their environments. Paragraph 9 states that new tourists "prefer accommodation arrangements such as cabins or camping. These types of accommodation, they believe, are more respectful of local culture."

12) The correct answer is D. "Affluent" means wealthy. The paragraph also uses the word "privileged," which implies that these tourists have a great deal of money.

13) The correct answer is A. The author expresses regret towards the past effects of tourism on the environment. We can assume that the author feels regret because the last paragraph claims that "all types of tourism should be responsible towards and respectful of environmental and human resources."

14) The correct answer is B. Paragraph 1 does not state that alcohol consumption has risen across many age groups in the last ten years. It merely points out that that there has been an increase in the consumption of alcoholic beverages by a particular group, namely, among the 11-to-15-year-old age group.

15) The correct answer is A. The best definition for the word *tackling* is trying to solve. We can understand this because other parts of the passage point out possible solutions.

16) The correct answer is C. The best explanation of the term health inequalities is that mortality and disease rates are greater for members of poor families. Paragraph 2 emphasizes that "rates of disease and death are far higher in poorer households."

17) The correct answer is D. The word "cynics" is synonymous with the word "doubters." In paragraph 3, we read that the cynics think that the "government's monetary support for poor households will invariably be spent on consumables like candy and potato chips, or other junk food, or worse, on tobacco, alcohol and even drugs." So, these people do not believe that the government can really help poor families.

18) The correct answer is C. The best place for the new sentence is at the end of paragraph 4. The new sentence states that "giving free school meals to children from lower-income families would be the best and most direct way of improving child nutrition." We know this is the best place because it relates to the "school breakfast and dinner programs" mentioned in the previous sentence in paragraph 4.

19) The correct answer is A. The word "they" refers to countries that have established school breakfasts. The previous sentence in paragraph 5 mentions that "some countries have developed programs for nutritious school breakfasts and dinners."

20) The correct answer is B. The best paraphrase is as follows: "Poor children do not start the day with a good meal and cannot learn well as a result, so it is of the utmost importance for the government to improve child poverty and child nutrition" The phrase "poor children do not start the day with a good meal and cannot learn well as a result" means the same as "disadvantaged children in many areas still do not get a nourishing breakfast and the effectiveness of their education is jeopardized as a result." The phrase "so it is of the utmost importance for the government to improve child poverty and child nutrition"

means the same thing as "there remains a clear need for the authorities to address nutrition as one of the worst symptoms of child poverty."

21) The correct answer is D. The author discusses smoking in paragraph 6 in order to expand on another aspect of poor health in children. We know this because the first sentence of paragraph 6 points out that "smoking also greatly damages the health of children and increases childhood mortality rates."

22) The correct answer is C. The main reason for the government's increase in the cigarette tax was to attempt to deter smoking, particularly by poor parents. Paragraph 6 states that the cigarette tax "has left poor parents who smoke worse off." So, we can assume that these poor parents have continued to smoke, and are now paying more for their smoking habit, thereby having less to spend on nutritious food.

23) The correct answer is B. The word "palatable" means tasty. We can understand this because paragraph 7 stresses that these drinks are sweet.

24) The correct answer is A. Based on paragraph 7, we can infer that the government is reluctant to criticize the practices of big businesses because it is loath to lose the monetary support that large beverage companies have to offer. "Loath" means "unwilling or reluctant".

25) The correct answer is D. The relationship between the goals of improved opportunities for children and the problems of child poverty and ill health is best described as follows: The achievement of the goal of the reduction of child poverty would improve child health and increase the opportunities of children to some extent, but it would not entirely eradicate the problem. Paragraph 8 states that "while these goals are related, it would be foolish to believe that the reduction of child poverty would automatically improve children's nutrition and reduce their smoking and drinking."

26) The correct answer is C. The author's main purpose in the passage is to enumerate the reasons for health inequalities, particularly in children, and to allude to some possible courses of action. Paragraph 4 mentions the solution of school breakfast and dinner programs. Paragraph 5 asserts that the "authorities [need] to address nutrition as one of the worst symptoms of child poverty." paragraph 6 claims that more government funds should be allocated to preventing cigarette sales to children. Finally, the last paragraph proposes "the allocation of governmental funds to nutrition and effective education."

27) The correct answer is C. The word "catalyst" in this passage is closest in meaning to "reason." We know that immigration is the reason because paragraph 1 states that the population has risen because immigration has increased.

28) The correct answer is B. The words "this steady influx" refer to the constant increase in people coming to the country for the first time. The previous paragraph describes how net inward migration increased during the study.

29) The correct answer is A. The most notable change to the population in the last one hundred years was the three-fold increase in the size of the population. Paragraph 3 clarifies that "notably, the population tripled from almost 76 million at the beginning of the twentieth century to nearly 281 million at the start of the twenty-first century."

30) The correct answer is B. The best place for the new sentence is in paragraph 3, which discusses changes to average household size.

31) The correct answer is D. The word "outstrip" in this passage is closest in meaning to the word "exceed." The paragraph states that "the population density of the Northeast . . . has always been high."

32) The correct answer is A. The author mentions the changes to the populations of Florida and Arizona to point out that new residents are continually moving to these states." Paragraph 3 mentions that "Florida and Arizona had the fastest-growing populations during the period of the study."

33) The correct answer is C. The phrase "lion's share of" is closest in meaning to "majority of." The sentence is talking about an increase in consumer credit, so we can surmise that credit cards are the primary cause for this phenomenon.

34) The correct answer is B. A possible interpretation is that the divorce rate went down because fewer people got married during the period of the study. The author's use of the word "concurrent" emphasizes that the decline in the marriage rate and the decrease in the divorce rate occurred at the same time.

35) The correct answer is D. The most notable demographic shift when comparing geographic areas was that many people moved from the Northeast and Midwest to live in the South or West. Paragraph 4 emphasizes that "until 1970 the majority of households were living in the Northeast and Midwest, but since 1980 the majority was in the South and West."

36) The correct answer is C. We can infer that women are more likely to live alone after losing a life partner than men are. Paragraph 4 points out that "female householders have increased as a proportion of all householders, and older females were far more likely to live alone than were men." We can infer that one of the primary reasons for living alone is losing one's life partner through death or breakup.

37) The correct answer is A. There has been a surge in consumer credit due to the reliance upon the use of credit cards to make purchases. The last paragraph suggests that "relatively worse-off households" use credit cards because they "struggle to make essential purchases."

38) The correct answer is A. Paragraphs 1 and 2 talk about how the population has increased as a result of immigration. Paragraphs 3 and 4 discuss notable changes in the concentration of the population in certain states and geographic regions, and paragraph 5 describes the way in which the distribution of income has become increasingly skewed in favor of the rich.

www.ingramcontent.com/pod-product-compliance
Lightning Source LLC
Chambersburg PA
CBHW081352080526
44588CB00016B/2462